THE CHESAPEAKE BAY

A Problem-Based Unit

The College of William and Mary
School of Education
Center for Gifted Education
Williamsburg, Virginia 23185

THE CHESAPEAKE BAY

A Problem-Based Unit

The College of William and Mary
School of Education
Center for Gifted Education
Williamsburg, Virginia 23185

Center for Gifted Education Staff:
Project Director: Dr. Joyce VanTassel-Baska
Project Managers: Dr. Shelagh A. Gallagher
Dr. Victoria B. Damiani
Project Consultants: Dr. Beverly T. Sher
Linda Neal Boyce
Dana T. Johnson
Dr. Jill D. Burruss
Donna L. Poland

Teacher Developers:
Barbara Weaver & Jeannette Adkins

funded by Jacob K. Javits,
United States Department of Education

KENDALL/HUNT PUBLISHING COMPANY
4050 Westmark Drive   Dubuque, Iowa 52002

CONTENTS

Part I

INTRODUCTORY FRAMEWORK

INTRODUCTION

The Chesapeake Bay is a problem-based science unit designed for high ability learners which has been successfully used with all learners in a wide variety of situations, from pull-out programs for gifted learners to traditional heterogeneously grouped classrooms. It allows middle school students to explore the ecosystem of the Bay in a novel way, namely through the process of grappling with an ill-structured, "real-world" problem.

Because the unit is problem-based, the way in which a teacher implements the unit will necessarily differ from the way in which most traditional science units are used. Preparing for and implementing problem-based learning takes time, flexibility, and a willingness to experiment with a new way of teaching.

The total time required for completion of *The Chesapeake Bay* should be minimally 30 hours, with more time required for additional activities.

RATIONALE AND PURPOSE

This unit has been designed to introduce high-ability sixth through eighth grade students to ecology and the impact of pollution on ecosystems by means of an examination of the Chesapeake Bay ecosystem. Although written with the Chesapeake Bay in mind, in principle it should be possible to adapt the activities contained in the unit to the study of other aquatic ecosystems as well.

The problem-based learning format was chosen in order to allow students to acquire significant science content knowledge in the course of solving an interdisciplinary, "real-world" problem. This format requires students to analyze the problem situation, to determine what information they need in order to come up with solutions, and then to find that information in a variety of ways. In addition to library work and other information-gathering methods, students, with teacher facilitation, perform experiments of their own design in order to find information necessary to come up with and evaluate solutions to the problem. The problem-based method also allows students to model the scientific process, from the problem-finding and information gathering steps through to the evaluation of experimental data and the recasting or solution of the problem.

Finally, the overarching scientific concept of systems is used as an organizing concept for the unit. The most important system in the unit is the Chesapeake Bay ecosystem; the impact of the economic and political systems on the Chesapeake Bay ecosystem is also a major focus of the unit.

GOALS AND OUTCOMES

> ➦ Goal: To understand the concept of systems

Students will be able to apply the ideas involved in the systems concept to the analysis of scientific systems, such as an ecosystem, and of other systems, such as the political and economic system.

SYSTEMS OUTCOMES

A. Students will be able to analyze several systems during the course of the unit. These include the "problem system" defined by the boundaries of the Chesapeake Bay; a local aquatic ecosystem; and the political system, at least as far as it affects the Chesapeake Bay.

B. For each system, students will be able to use appropriate systems language to identify boundaries, important elements, input, and output.

C. Students will be able to analyze the interactions of various system components with each other and with input into the system.

D. Based on their understanding of the Chesapeake Bay ecosystem, students will be able to predict the impact of various kinds of input (point and nonpoint pollution sources, new government regulations, and so on) on the Chesapeake Bay.

E. Students will analyze issues surrounding human impact on the Bay to their peers.

> ➦ Goal: To design scientific experiments necessary to solve given problems

SCIENTIFIC PROCESS OUTCOMES

A. Students will explore a new scientific area, namely the Chesapeake Bay ecosystem.

B. Students will be able to identify meaningful scientific problems for investigation during the course of working through the problem and its ramifications.

C. During their experimental work, students will:

—Demonstrate good data-handling skills

—Analyze any experimental data as appropriate

—Evaluate their results in light of the original problem

—Use their enhanced understanding of the area under study to make predictions about similar problems whose answers are not yet known to the student

—Communicate their enhanced understanding of the scientific area to others

➥ Goal: To learn about aquatic ecosystems

Students will acquire a general understanding of the nature and properties of ecosystems.

SPECIFIC CONTENT OUTCOMES

A. Students will be able to analyze the Chesapeake Bay ecosystem in detail, with attention to biotic and abiotic elements, interactions between these elements, and the effects of human activity on the system.

B. Students will be able to investigate the life cycles of a number of different Bay organisms and use their understanding of these organisms to predict the effects of various perturbations in the Bay, either natural or anthropogenic.

C. Students will become familiar with water testing procedures and their uses in detecting pollution.

D. Students will be able to investigate the factors that maximize algal growth.

E. Students will be able to analyze the water quality of a nearby aquatic ecosystem, and investigate the organisms present.

ASSESSMENT

This unit contains many assessment opportunities that can be used to monitor student progress and assess student learning. Opportunities for formative assessment include:

- The student's problem log, a written compilation of the student's thoughts about the problem. Each lesson contains suggested questions for students to answer in their problem logs. The problem log should also be used by the student to record data and new information that they have obtained during the course of the unit.

- Experimental design worksheets, which can be used to assess a student's understanding of experimental design and the scientific process, as well as to record information about what was done and what was found during student-directed experimentation.

- Other forms, such as the Field Trip Data Sheet, which are used to help the student explain their solutions to particular parts of the problem.

- Teacher observation of student participation in large-group and small-group activities.

Opportunities for cumulative assessment include:

- The final resolution activity, which involves a small group presentation of a solution to the unit's ill-structured problem; the quality of the solution will reflect the group's understanding of the science involved as well as the societal and ethical considerations needed to form an acceptable solution. This activity requires each group to prepare a written report detailing and justifying their solution, which can be used for assessment purposes as well.

- The Bayfest activity in which students use their understanding of the Bay and human activities that affect the Bay to educate their peers.

- Final unit assessments, which allow the teacher to determine whether individual students have met the science process, science content, and systems objectives listed in the Goals and Objectives section at the beginning of the unit.

Safety Precautions to Be Taken in the Lab

As this unit involves laboratory work, some general safety procedures should be observed at all times. Some districts will have prescribed laboratory safety rules; for those that do not, some basic rules to follow for this unit and any other curriculum involving scientific experimentation are:

1. Students must behave appropriately in the lab. No running or horseplay should be allowed; materials should be used for only the intended purposes.

2. No eating, drinking, or smoking in lab; no tasting of laboratory materials. No pipetting by mouth.

3. If students are using heat sources, such as alcohol burners, long hair must be tied back and loose clothing should be covered by a lab coat.

4. Fire extinguishers should be available; students should know where they are and how to use them.

Some specific safety rules relevant to implementing this unit:

1. Students will obey all school rules at all times in class, on the bus, and at all outside study areas.

2. Students will stay with their partners or teams and in the assigned areas on all trips.

3. Parents should be aware of any outside field trips and have students appropriately dressed for field work. Upon returning, parents should check students for ticks and watch for signs of poison ivy. Teacher should inform students and parents of appropriate "field dress."

4. Students should be reminded to respect and appreciate all life forms—disregard for life (plant and animal) will not be tolerated. Unnecessary destruction of habitat (pulling up plants, etc.) while on outside field trip will not be tolerated.

MATERIALS LIST

Materials needed for each individual lesson are listed in the "Materials and Handouts" section of the lesson.

LESSON FLOW CHART

Problem-based learning is not easy to plan, because it is driven by student questioning and interest. We have included estimated durations for each lesson in this unit, but be prepared to be flexible and to move with the students. We have also included a diagram (Figure 1) which shows the relationship between the individual lessons and experiments suggested in the unit. In general, lessons shown higher in the diagram are prerequisites for those shown lower in the diagram. Be aware that this diagram may not reflect all of the time that you will need to spend; students may well come up with unanticipated, yet valid, experiments or lines of questioning.

TAILORING *THE CHESAPEAKE BAY* TO YOUR LOCATION

Classroom experience during the unit piloting process has shown that this unit is much more powerful when tailored for the location in which it is being presented. Some general considerations in localizing the Bay problem include:

1. Choose a water system that includes the region where your school is located. Check with local experts to see what fish or other aquatic cuisine is currently experiencing a decline in population.

2. Use local maps of the water system. These include highway maps, topographic maps, landsat maps, etc. Check with local government offices to see what kinds of maps are available.

3. Involve local experts (fish and game department, agriculture extension office, farmers, gardeners, biologists, fishermen, etc.) as speakers and on-going resources in the problem-solving process.

4. Visit a part of the water system where the endangered species lives to observe the local ecosystem and sample the water.

FIGURE 1

LESSON FLOW CHART

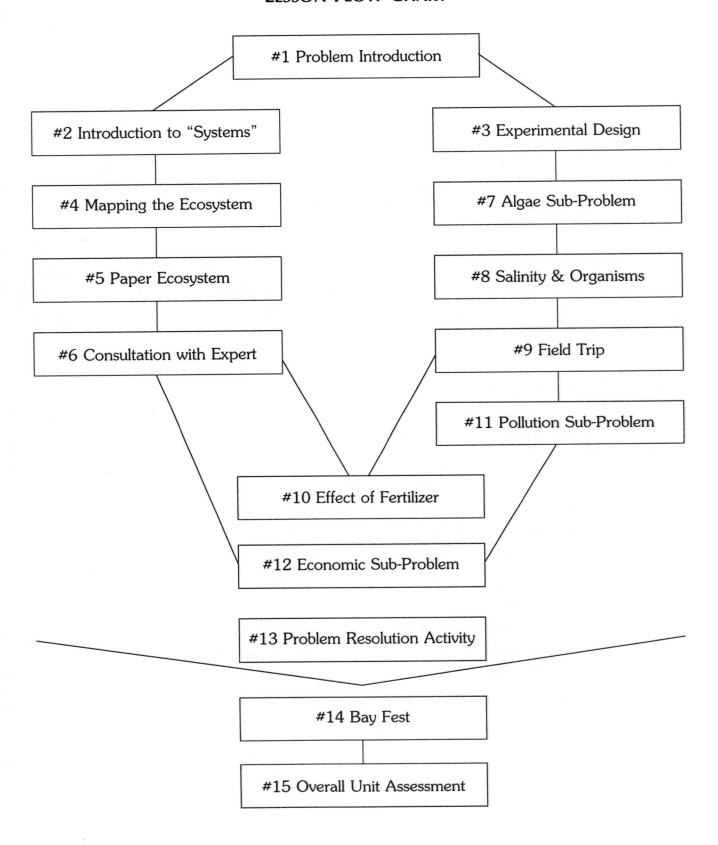

5. Work with librarians to plan the unit and to assist students in finding information. In addition to school librarians and academic librarians, special libraries (museums, corporations, historical societies, etc.) offer vast resources relevant to the unit.

This customization has several potential advantages: the site is familiar to the students, there are real, detailed topographic and street maps available, and the students can talk to the actual people who would be involved in managing such a spill.

Below is an example of a tailored problem done by Docia Jones, a 6th grade teacher in Lexington School District #4, South Carolina:

> As a boy, Josh and Julie Miller's grandfather had fond memories of camping in the Congaree Swamp, and fishing in Weston Lake. They would catch Black Bass and Bream, clean them and cook them over the campfire. Grandpa Miller said those were the best tasting fish he had ever eaten.
>
> Grandpa Miller took Julie and Josh fishing in Western Lake. Grandpa showed them how to catch and clean the fish as he had done when he was a boy. However, when they fried the fish and hungrily began eating them, Josh and Julie found they tasted terrible. Not wanting to hurt Grandpa's feelings, they said nothing, but when Grandpa tasted the fish, he said, "These fish aren't fit to eat! They have a really strange taste."
>
> Grandpa asked the park naturalist if he ever fished in Weston Lake and he said, "We don't eat those fish anymore. The flavor of the fish has changed over the last five years. There does not seem to be as many as there used to be, either." Grandpa was upset. "What is happening here? I thought that when they made our swamp a national monument, all of its resources would be protected," he said.
>
> Josh and Julie are understandably upset by this event. Wondering why the fish are fewer and are tasting bad, they decide to investigate. You are Josh and Julie's science teacher and they are your favorite students. They have come to ask for your help in their investigations. How can you help Josh and Julie?

GLOSSARY OF TERMS

Abiotic: Nonliving component of the environment including soil, water, air, light, nutrients, and the like.

Algae/Algal Growth: The increased growth of any various chiefly aquatic, eukanyotic, photosynthetic organisms, ranging in size from single celled forms to the giant kelp.

Best Management Practices (BMP): These include temporary construction methods like silt fencing and curb drop inlet protection to prevent sediment from washing into area waterways. They also refer to more permanent structures such as grassy swales, retention or detention ponds, and rock beds to naturally filter storm water runoff.

Boundary (Systems): Something that indicates or fixes a limit on the extent of the system.

Biotic and Abiotic Input: From the areas outside their boundaries both living and non-living (animals that immigrate, sunlight, rain, pollutants).

Biotic: All living organisms that live within their boundaries.

Ecosystem: The ecological community together with its environment, functioning as a unit.

Element (Systems): A distinct part of the system; a component of a complex entity (system).

Fertilizer: Any of a large number of natural and synthetic materials, including manure and nitrogen, phosphorus, and potassium compounds, spread or worked into soil to increase its capacity to support plant growth.

Fertilization: The act or process of applying a fertilizer.

Input (Systems): Something that is put in the system; an addition to the components of the system.

Interactions: The nature of reciprocal connections made between/among elements and inputs of a system.

Output: Products emanating from a system (e.g., oxygen, carbon dioxide, waste products, creatures that emigrate or are taken out of the ecosystem).

Point and Nonpoint Source Pollution: There are generally two types of water pollution addressed by regulations. One source is specific. An industrial leak or hazardous material dump is called a "point source" pollution. The other is very broad and is generated in many ways and from many sources. "Nonpoint" source pollution includes oil, grease, lawn chemicals, detergents, litter, yard and pet waste, soil erosion, etc. The second type is targeted by local programs such as storm water management, septic system pumpout and the Chesapeake Bay Preservation District Regulations, etc.

Pollutant: Something that pollutes, especially a waste material that contaminates air, soil, or water.

Pollution: The act of discharging harmful pollutants.

Scientific Process (or Research): The scientific research process can be described by the following steps:

1. Learn a great deal about your field.
2. Think of a good (interesting, important, and tractable) problem.

3. Decide which experiments/observations/calculations would contribute to a solution of the problem.

4. Perform the experiments/observations/calculations.

5. Decide whether the results really do contribute to a better understanding of the problem. If they do not, return to either step 2 (if you're very discouraged) or step 3. If they do, go to step 6.

6. Communicate your results to as many people as possible. If they're patentable, tell your lawyer before you tell anyone else, and write a patent application or two. Publish them in a scientific journal (or if they are really neat, in *The New York Times*); go to conferences and talk about them; tell all of your friends.

System: A group of interacting, interrelated, or interdependent elements forming a complex whole.

LETTER TO PARENTS

Dear Parent or Guardian:

Your child is about to begin a science unit that uses an instructional strategy called problem-based learning. In this unit students will take a very active role in identifying and resolving a "real-world" problem constructed to promote science learning. Your child will not be working out of a textbook during this unit but will be gathering information from a variety of other sources both in and out of school.

The goals for the unit are:

• To understand the concept of "systems."

> Students will be able to analyze several systems during the course of the unit. These include the "problem system" defined by the boundaries of the Chesapeake Bay; a local aquatic ecosystem; and the economic and political systems affecting the Chesapeake Bay.

• To learn about aquatic ecosystems.

> Students will be able to analyze the Chesapeake Bay ecosystem in detail, will be able to investigate the life cycles of a number of different Bay organisms, and will use their understanding of these organisms to predict the effects of various natural and man-made changes in the Bay ecosystem.

• To design scientific experiments necessary to solve given problems.

> In order to solve given scientific problems, students will design, perform, and report on the results of a number of experiments. During their experimental work, students will first identify a meaningful scientific question; design an experiment to address this scientific question; perform their experiment; and record their data and observations appropriately. They will then analyze and manipulate their data as appropriate and report on their results. Finally, they will evaluate their experiment and its results, both from the point of view of the original scientific question and from the point of view of the applicability of their new understanding to the larger problem set up in the unit.

Since we know from educational research that parental involvement is a strong factor in promoting positive attitudes toward science, we encourage you to extend your child's school learning through activities in the home.

Ways that you may wish to help your child during the learning of this unit include:

• Discuss the concept of systems, including family systems, educational systems, etc.

• Discuss the problem they have been given.

- Engage your child in scientific-experimentation exercises based on everyday events such as: In a grocery store, how would you test whether it's better to go in a long line with people having few items or a short line with people having full carts?

- Take your child to area science museums and the library to explore how scientists solve problems.

- Use the problem-based learning model to query students about a question they may have about the real world, e.g., How does hail form? What do you know about hail? What do you need to know to answer the question? How do you find out?

Thank you in advance for your interest in your child's curriculum. Please do not hesitate to contact me for further information as the unit progresses.

Sincerely,

Part II

LESSON

PLANS

Problem Introduction

LESSON LENGTH: 2 sessions

INSTRUCTIONAL PURPOSE

- To introduce students to the problem statement to be explored throughout the unit.

MATERIALS AND HANDOUTS

Handout 1.1: Problem Statement
  Handout 1.2: "Need to Know" board
  Handout 1.3: Problem Log Question
Handout 1.4: Problem Web

Session 1

THINGS TO DO

1. Read the problem statement to students (see attached copy). Have students identify key words and phrases as they organize the elements of the problem. Use the "Need to Know" board to help students identify what they know and what they need to know.

2. Organize the problem statement into three categories on the "Need to Know" board: What Do We Know, What Do We Need To Know, and How Can We Find Out. Prioritize the Need to Know list from most to least critical.

3. Debate reasons for prioritizing choices. Ask students to identify resources that will help them answer or further investigate the elements of the Need to Know list. Divide the learning issues among students so that each student (or a different group of students) will bring different information to the class on the following session.

THINGS TO ASK

- What's going on?

- What are we supposed to do?

- What seems to be the main problem?

- Is this a problem specific to the restaurant?

- Why might sea trout be unavailable at the restaurant?

- Where else might they go to find sea trout?

- Are there other problems?

- Where can we find the answers to these questions?

Session 2

THINGS TO DO

Have students report the information that they found. Look back over the "Need to Know" list and identify: 1) what questions they have answered; and 2) what new questions arise out of their new information. Next, ask students what they are going to need to know in order to solve the problem. Prioritize the list based on negotiations with students.

THINGS TO ASK

- What questions are answered by the new information?

- What questions do we still have to answer?

- What new questions do you have?

- What are the things we may have to learn about to solve the problem?

- Is the problem different today than it was yesterday?

- How are we going to solve this problem?

ASSESSMENT

1. Paraphrase of the problem situation in the problem log.
2. Problem Web.

EXTENSION: CHESAPEAKE HORIZONS

The question of pollution will be a major part of students' initial research. Focus on that question through the viewing of the video "Chesapeake Horizons" from the Chesapeake Bay Foundation.

PROBLEM STATEMENT

Julie and Josh Miller's grandfather has come back to Virginia for one of his periodic visits. While eating with the family in Sam's Restaurant in the Phoebus section of Hampton, Grandfather Miller is very upset to find that sea trout is no longer on the menu.

"I came here to eat sea trout because Sam is the only one who can prepare it the way it should be cooked! Let me talk to Sam about this!" exclaims Grandfather Miller. When informed that Sam is on vacation in Florida, Grandfather becomes more angry and it is with great effort that the Millers convince him to settle for flounder stuffed with crab meat instead of sea trout.

Julie and Josh are understandably upset by these events. Wondering why sea trout is not available for their grandfather, they decide to investigate.

You are Julie and Josh's science teacher; they are your favorite students. They've come to ask for your help in their investigation. How can you help Julie and Josh?

The Chesapeake Bay

HANDOUT 1.2

"NEED TO KNOW" BOARD

What do we know?	What do we need to know?	How can we find out?

HANDOUT 1.3

PROBLEM LOG QUESTIONS

1. After our first couple of days of discussion, what do you think the problem really is?

2. Why do you think this is the main problem?

3. Is it the same problem you thought is was when we first started talking?

4. How has it changed?

5. What are the issues you are most interested in finding out about?

HANDOUT 1.4

PROBLEM WEB

Place the central problem statement in the circle in the center of the page (summarize if you have to). Using this as your central focus point, create a web showing the relationships among various parts of the problem.*

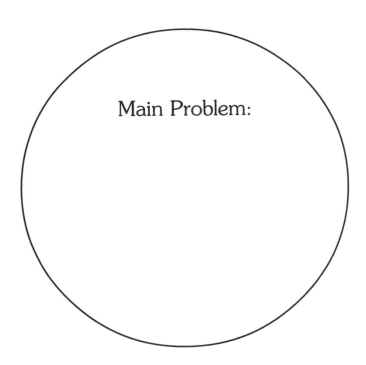

Main Problem:

*If students are unfamiliar with concept mapping, teachers should create an example in class prior to giving this assignment.

lesson 2

Introduction to "Systems"

LESSON LENGTH: 1 session

INSTRUCTIONAL PURPOSE

- To introduce students to the concept of "systems."

MATERIALS AND HANDOUTS

Fishbowl
Water
Pebbles
Fish (more than one!)
Fish food

Handout 2.1: System Parts Chart
Handout 2.2: Goldfish Bowl
Handout 2.3: Problem Log Questions

THINGS TO DO

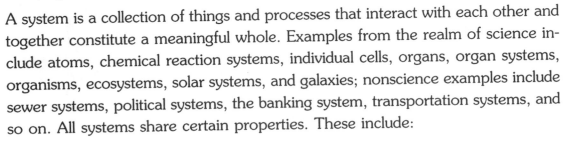

1. Ask students in small groups to come up with several examples of a system. Then have them categorize their examples and discuss.

2. Ask students to cite examples of non-systems. Then have them generalize about their understanding of systems. (Students should be able to describe a system as made up of elements and movement.)

A system is a collection of things and processes that interact with each other and together constitute a meaningful whole. Examples from the realm of science include atoms, chemical reaction systems, individual cells, organs, organ systems, organisms, ecosystems, solar systems, and galaxies; nonscience examples include sewer systems, political systems, the banking system, transportation systems, and so on. All systems share certain properties. These include:

a. Systems have identifiable elements.

b. Systems have definable boundaries.

c. Most systems receive input in the form of material or information from outside their boundaries and generate output to the world outside their boundaries.

d. The interactions of a system's elements with each other and their response to input from outside the system combine to determine the overall nature and behavior of the system.

3. Looking at an empty fishbowl, describe a boundary and ask what the boundary would be for some fish living together in the bowl.

4. Have a student pour some water into the fishbowl and ask if the boundary for where the fish might live has changed.

5. Add more water until the bowl is full and ask again about the changing boundary. Is any part of the fishbowl constant? Have students write a definition of boundaries for a system on their System Parts Chart.

6. Add fish and discuss the elements in a system of fish living together in the fishbowl.

7. Describe input (e.g., light, food) and output (e.g., dirty water) of a fishbowl system. Students can add definitions of these terms to their System Parts Chart (Handout 2.1).

8. Talk about interactions (e.g., fish and plants, light and plants, fish and food) within a fishbowl system. Students can add descriptions to their System Parts Chart.

9. Provide situations that would put stress on the system: if there were six goldfish in the bowl, or if insufficient food were added to the system or if a pregnant guppy were added, but no additional food. What would happen to the system elements, input, output and interactions in those cases. Introduce the idea of natural regulation in the system (that the amount of oxygen regulates the number of fish).

10. Be sure that the definition and all generalizations used to frame the unit are discussed in relationship to student-generated ones.

THINGS TO ASK

- What is contained in the fishbowl?
- Is the pencil on your desk part of the fishbowl system? Why?
- What else might be an element in a fishbowl system?
- Could there be other elements?

- What happens if we add things to the fishbowl?
- Do all fishbowl systems have the same boundary, elements, input and output?
- What would happen to the system if (stressing situation here)?
- What are the things that determine how many goldfish will survive in the bowl?
- How do these things help to keep the system in balance?
- How are regulating factors in the system like our laws?
- How could knowing about systems help us understand our problem better?

ASSESSMENT

1. Ask students why knowing about systems is important to the Bay problem.
2. Draw a diagram of the Bay indicating boundaries, elements, inputs, outputs, interactions.
3. Describe three ways that the system regulates itself.
4. Describe what would happen if one of those regulatory mechanisms was stressed beyond its endurance.
5. Problem Log Question: Describe pollution in relation to the regulation system of the Bay.

The Chesapeake Bay

HANDOUT 2.1

SYSTEMS PARTS CHART

1. What are the boundaries of the system? Why did you choose them? Were there other possibilities?

2. List some important elements of the system.

3. Describe input into the system. Where does it come from?

4. Describe output from the system. What part(s) of the system produce it?

5. Describe some important interactions:
   a. among system elements

   b. between system elements and input into the system.

6. What would happen to the system if the interactions in 5a could not take place? In 5b?

The Chesapeake Bay

HANDOUT 2.2

GOLDFISH BOWL

Name: _____

Draw some elements, input and output of the goldfish bowl and label them. Make sure you put them in the right spot in the system. Then label the boundaries of the goldfish bowl.

What are some interactions that happen in this system?

HANDOUT 2.3

PROBLEM LOG QUESTIONS

Describe the problem we have defined in the context of a system. What is wrong with the system?

Introduction to Experimental Design*

LESSON LENGTH: 1 session

INSTRUCTIONAL PURPOSE

- To introduce students to experimental design and related terms: hypothesis, variables, controls, repeated trials, constants, analysis of data, results.
- To investigate the effect of calcium chloride on the temperature of water.

MATERIALS AND HANDOUTS

150ml beaker or plastic cup (4 per group)

Thermometer (°C)

One teaspoon scoop or spoon

Chemical (calcium chloride)‡

Sodium chloride (common salt—non-iodized variety)

Clock or timer

Water (distilled or tap)—be consistent (don't use both types of water unless the students are experimenting on the impact of different types of water on effect)

Graduated cylinder

Wooden stick or plastic straw for stirring

‡Calcium chloride is used to prevent icing of walkways and roads. It is available through hardware and agricultural suppliers, as well as chemical vendors.

Handout 3.1: Problem Log Questions

SAFETY

Wear goggles

Wash hands

Dispose of chemicals in marked containers

*Adapted from: Cothron, J.H., Giese, R.N., & Rezba, R.J. (1996). *Students and research: Practical strategies for science classrooms and competition.* Dubuque, IA: Kendall/Hunt Publishing Company.

NOTE TO TEACHER

1. Review how to read thermometers.
2. Review with students the correct procedure for mixing or agitating solutions.

THINGS TO DO

1. Talk to students about safety procedures (or the lab activity). Show students the substances that they will be working with during the lab activity. Ask students to list precautions that would protect their skin, eyes, and clothing; these precautions should include both proper behavior during the activity and necessary safety equipment. Write the list of "lab safety rules" on the chalk board or butcher paper so everyone can see it during lab.

2. Divide students into 4 teams (5 if necessary). Give each team a beaker or a cup with about $1/3$ cup or 75ml of room temperature tap or distilled water.

3. Pass out thermometers and stirring utensils. Have students record the temperature of the stirred water in each cup.

4. Calcium chloride will be the independent variable that is going to be manipulated first in the system.

5. Have students add the designated amount of chemicals and stir (agitate) the solution for 2 minutes. You may need to time this part of the experiment if at least one student in each group doesn't have a watch with a second hand.

6. At the end of the 2 minutes, have students measure and record the temperature.

Amt. of Chemical 1 level tsp.	Initial Temperature	Ending Temperature	Change in Temperature
0			
1			
2			
3			

7. Calculate the temperature change.

8. Record data on a class data table. (Your table may reflect more than 3 trials if you have more teams.)

Amount of Chemical	Change in Temperature (°C) Trials			Average Change in Temperature (°C)
	1	2	3	
0				
1				
2				
3				

9. Average the change in temperature (°C).

10. Clean out beaker (cups) and redo with sodium chloride. Have the student hypothesize possible results.

11. Record results on a second class data table. (Your table may reflect more than 3 trials if you have more teams.)

12. Clean up activity area and have students come back for a discussion of the results. Compare the findings from each chemical experiment.

THINGS TO ASK

Before the activity:

- Have you seen calcium chloride before? How was it used?

- If this is a system, what effect do you think adding calcium chloride (an input) will have on the temperature of the water? (State a *hypothesis*. If this . . ., then this . . . will occur.)

After the activity:

- Why were measurements made on water containing 0 scoops of calcium chloride? (Detect hidden variables that might effect H_2O change.)

- How accurate is the temperature measurement?

- What was the independent variable (the variable that we manipulated)?

- What was the dependent variable (the variable that was affected by the independent variable)?

- Was our hypothesis correct?
- Could we have done this experiment better?
- What changes would you make? Why?
- What things remained constant?
- Why were repeated trials necessary?
- What if we conducted only one trial?
- What was the difference using sodium chloride? Why was there a difference?
- How did the second experiment compare to the first?
- Was our hypothesis correct? Why or why not?

Problem-related questions:

- How is this experiment like the goldfish system?
- What are the inputs? Outputs? Boundaries? (Relate to goldfish system.)
- Do you think these situations (addition of calcium chloride to H_2O) might occur in our environment? (Additions of sodium chloride to water.)
- What effect do you think they might have? Why?
- Are there other effects that might occur that we didn't measure today? What might they be?

ASSESSMENT

Problem Log Questions

NOTE TO TEACHER

This experiment needs to be repeated for each solution type three different times. You may wish to give each group four cups and have them conduct the experiment using one cup for each variation in calcium chloride addition. (This type of organization seems to work best.) Or you may want to have one group look at a certain calcium chloride amount in three different cups. In either case, each group should have one cup for control (no scoops added). Each group would conduct the experimental procedure on each cup only once. A class chart would reflect the "repeated trials," which are needed.

HANDOUT 3.1

PROBLEM LOG QUESTIONS

1. What are the basic concepts of experimental design, variables, constants, control, repeated trials, and hypothesis, in the experiments we just completed? How can identifying these basic concepts in any experiment help you to improve that experiment?

2. List and describe the safety procedures we discussed in class today. Include both safety equipment and safe behaviors. After today's activity, do you think we need to add more to the list? Why or why not? If yes, what are they? Are any of our rules unnecessary? If yes, which ones and why?

lesson

4

Mapping and Understanding the Ecosystem

LESSON LENGTH: 2–3 sessions

INSTRUCTIONAL PURPOSE

- To use geography skills and topics to help students understand the Bay ecosystem.*

MATERIALS AND HANDOUTS

Handouts 4.1–4.4: Assignment sheets for groups

Resource materials, including but not limited to:
encyclopedia, atlas, geography books, maps, almanac etc.

Presentation materials, including but not limited to:
chart paper, graph paper, markers, tape, etc.

THINGS TO DO

1. Each group is assigned to describe the Chesapeake Bay ecosystem based on a specific geography topic. Divide the class into four groups; give each group a different topic information sheet:

   Group 1: Location/physical characteristics

   Group 2: Environment

   Group 3: Human interaction

   Group 4: Changes in the Bay region over time

2. Students use the handout as a guide to explore each geography topic through the skills of asking and answering geographic questions and through acquiring, organizing, and analyzing geographic information. They can also ask questions of the teacher or explore available resources to further understand the geography theme definitions.

*Referenced to Grades 5–8 geographic skills, p. 50 in *National Geography Standards* (1994). *Geography for Life*. Washington, DC: National Geographic Research and Exploration.

3. Ask each group to prepare an illustrated presentation of the Chesapeake Bay ecosystem using the theme it has been assigned.

4. Group presentations will probably require one to two sessions. Groups should: 1) explain their topic to the class based on their assigned work; 2) describe and illustrate the Chesapeake Bay ecosystem according to their assigned topic; and 3) explain how they think their description of the Chesapeake Bay might help (or hinder) the resolution of the sea trout problem.

THINGS TO ASK

- How were all of the descriptions of the Chesapeake Bay ecosystem different? What were the common elements?

- Did any one presentation give a complete description of the Bay?

- How did the descriptions help us to understand the Chesapeake Bay in different ways?

- How does the geography of the Chesapeake Bay region affect its ecosystem?

- How might the different descriptions help us with our problem?

- Do these descriptions affect the way we think of the (elements, inputs, outputs, boundaries, interactions) of the Chesapeake Bay ecosystem?

ASSESSMENT

Geography presentations.

HANDOUT 4.1

GROUP 1
LOCATION/PHYSICAL CHARACTERISTICS

1. Determine the location of the Chesapeake Bay. Use latitude and longitude as one determination of location. Then look at the location of the Bay relative to geographic features that are found nearby. These include rivers, ocean, cities, mountains, land masses, etc. What possible influences might they have on the Bay? What might these characteristics mean for the sea trout problem?

2. Draw or create something to teach the group about the location of the Bay and its physical characteristics and their possible importance for the problem.

HANDOUT 4.2

GROUP 2
ENVIRONMENT

1. What kinds of organisms live in the Bay region? What do they eat? What eats them? Which of them are a food source for humans? What role does wetland habitat play in this food chain? How is the water in the Bay different from the ocean and its tributaries? What are the connections of the Bay to the global ecosystem?

2. Draw or create something to teach the group about the environment of the Bay and its possible importance for the problem.

GROUP 3
HUMAN INTERACTIONS

1. Determine the patterns of human settlement in the Chesapeake Bay region. What are the transportation patterns that have developed in the region to facilitate local travel and global travel? What are the imports and exports that are important to the region? What kinds of industries are located in this area (factories, agriculture, military, recreation, etc.)? How do they use the Bay and what effects do they have on it? Do any of the population centers in the region draw their water supply from the Bay or its tributaries?

2. Draw or create something to teach the group about how human interactions affect the Bay region and their possible importance for the problem.

HANDOUT 4.4

GROUP 4
CHANGES IN THE BAY REGION OVER TIME

1. Many changes have taken place in the Chesapeake Bay region over both long and short periods of time. Look for information about long term changes such as geologic changes, land use patterns, deforestation, erosion, water temperature, etc. Also consider the effects of short term changes such as floods, hurricanes, drought, and algae blooms.

2. Draw or create something to teach the group about elements of change that have affected the Bay or do affect the Bay and their possible importance for the problem.

lesson 5

Paper Ecosystem

LESSON LENGTH: 3 sessions

INSTRUCTIONAL PURPOSE

- To reinforce students' understanding of a system and the parts of the Bay ecosystem specifically.

MATERIALS AND HANDOUTS

Overhead projector
Overhead projector overlays of topographic map
Transparency markers
Index cards
Colored string
Topographic map of the Bay region

Handout 5.1: Organisms Studied
Handout 5.2: Problem Log Questions
Handout 5.3: Constructing a Paper Ecosystem

THINGS TO DO

1. Discuss the overall concept of systems, reviewing the following components of the ecosystem:

   boundaries   biotic and abiotic input

   biotic elements   output

   abiotic elements   elements

2. Work with students to help them create a paper ecosystem designed to be the most helpful representation for the purposes of solving the sea trout problem (see directions on Teacher Support 5.3).

THINGS TO ASK

- What descriptive information have you gathered about the Bay?
- Which of these components would you categorize as elements, inputs, outputs, boundaries?
- Which components are biotic? Which are abiotic?
- In a system, are the boundaries fixed absolutely, or are they arbitrary? Why? How can you tell?
- How would you want to represent the Bay ecosystem for the purposes of solving our problem?
- Which of the information we categorized would be absolutely essential?

ASSESSMENT

1. Ability of students to construct and describe the paper ecosystem.
2. Problem Log

NOTE TO TEACHER

You should consider coming back to the paper ecosystem several times throughout the unit to see if students want to alter the system as they understand the problem better. In this respect, it parallels the problem web activity.

The
Chesapeake
Bay

Handout 5.1

Organisms Studied

Have students make a list of organisms that live in the Bay. Each student should be assigned one or more organisms for the purpose of gathering the following information:

A. Where in the ecosystem does the organism live? (On the shore, near the shore, in the deep waters of the Bay, in the mud at the bottom of the Bay.)

B. What does the organism eat? Does it need different kinds of food in the different parts of its life cycle?

C. What creatures eat the organism? Does it have different predators at different times in its life cycle?

D. What is the organism's life cycle like? (When and where does it reproduce, does it migrate?)

E. At different times in its life cycle, does the organism need any special range of temperatures, pH levels, or concentrations of dissolved nutrients?

HANDOUT 5.2

PROBLEM LOG QUESTIONS

1. Why is the ecosystem you created the best representation for the problem?

2. Describe one change you could make to the boundaries of your ecosystem and the effect that change would have on the system as a whole.

HANDOUT 5.3

CONSTRUCTING A PAPER ECOSYSTEM

STEP 1. DEFINE THE BOUNDARIES OF THE ECOSYSTEM

Students should reach consensus on what needs to be inside or outside of their ecosystem. For example, the ecosystem of the Chesapeake Bay could be strictly construed to include only the water that is physically inside the Bay; on the other hand, if sea trout are the organisms that they are most interested in, then the waters of the estuaries adjacent to the Bay should be included, as well as any river waters that the sea trout use for spawning or other purposes. It is worthwhile for students to realize that system boundaries can be optimized for the study of some particular problem: in the Chesapeake Bay problem, defining the boundaries of the system to include the waters mentioned above but NOT the adjacent farmland and cities means that the elements making up those adjacent areas do not need to be considered except as they produce input into the system that is the Bay and adjacent waters; on the other hand, the entire sea trout environment (except for the environment of those fish that enter the ocean) is present for analysis within the system's boundaries.

STEP 2. FIND OUT ABOUT THE ELEMENTS OF THE SYSTEM

Have students make a list of organisms that live in the Bay. Each student should be assigned one or more organisms for the purpose of gathering the following information:

A. Where in the ecosystem does the organism live? (On the shore, near the shore, in the deep waters of the Bay, in the mud at the bottom of the Bay.)

B. What does the organism eat? Does it need different kinds of food in the different parts of its life cycle?

C. What creatures eat the organism? Does it have different predators at different times in its life cycle?

D. What is the organism's life cycle like? (When and where does it reproduce, does it migrate?)

E. At different times in its life cycle, does the organism need any special range of temperatures, pH levels, or concentrations of dissolved nutrients?

This sort of information can be obtained from field guides, encyclopedias, and books about natural history.

STEP 3. ASSEMBLING THE ECOSYSTEM

A. Obtain a topographic map of the territory occupied by the ecosystem. Have students plot the range of their organism on overhead projector overlay copies of the topo map; if the range is not available, ask them to predict where the organism can be found based on the information that they have about its lifestyle. If the range of their organism also depends on factors such as salinity of the water, ask them to predict where the water of appropriate salinity would be found and use their prediction to plot their organism's range. If their organism's range varies depending on time of year or stage of its life cycle, ask the student to indicate this with different colors on their map. When students have finished, they can easily see whether two organisms can interact directly by placing the two maps on top of each other. This also illustrates the effects of geography and abiotic factors on the behavior of the biotic elements of an ecosystem.

B. Have students put the name of their organism on an index card. Staple each index card to the bulletin board, being sure to leave lots of space between the index cards. Then, have students connect predators with prey by attaching the opposite ends of a piece of string to each member of a predator-prey pair. If a particular predator or prey organism is not among those already present, have the student add an index card to the display with the organism's name on it. When students have finished, they will have created a physical representation of a food web, and thus illustrated some of the kinds of biotic interactions that go on in an ecosystem. Keep a photographic record of all this data.

C. Abiotic factors: Have students make a master list of all of the abiotic elements of the ecosystem. Put this master list next to the food web on the bulletin board. Then, have students use strings to connect each abiotic factor that directly affects their organism to the index card with their organism's name on it. A new color of string could be used to distinguish abiotic/biotic element interactions from those already present in the food web. Photographically record this as well.

STEP 4: INPUT AND OUTPUT

Ask students to list the different kinds of input and output that the ecosystem receives/generates. Ask them to diagram this individually or in small groups.

STEP 5: INTERACTIONS

Ask each student to predict the direct effects of a specific environmental perturbation on their organism. For example, if the water level in the estuary drops dramatically thanks to a severe drought, will their organism be directly affected? Why? Then, have them use a single color of pen (everyone uses red, for example) to indicate the effects of this perturbation on the index card that denotes their animal on the bulletin board (an arrow up for an increase in the population, an arrow down for a decrease in the population, and no arrow for no change will do nicely.) Second-order effects can then be determined by having each student look at what has happened to its organism's predators and prey and predicting how its organism's population will respond in a new color of pen. The rippling-through of a single perturbation can be modeled by this activity.

lesson 6

Consultation with an Expert on Bay Ecology

LESSON LENGTH: 3 sessions

INSTRUCTIONAL PURPOSE

- To provide interaction with a professional working on Bay ecology.

MATERIALS AND HANDOUTS

Chart and markers

Audio-visual equipment for guest speaker

Handout 6.1: Visitor Planning Sheet

Session 1: Before the Speaker Comes

THINGS TO DO

1. Brainstorm with students, deciding what questions need to be asked of the speaker. Use the "Need to Know" board to choose questions.

2. Class discussion can help sort questions into most and least important questions.

3. Students should also be guided to think about the best way to phrase the questions. Are they specific enough? Are they too specific?

4. Group questions can be recorded on a master question chart.

5. Students can then add any of their own questions to individual Visitor Planning Sheets (Handout 6.1).

THINGS TO ASK

- What information do we want to know?
- What information will the guest speaker be most qualified to give?
- What do we want to know by the time the guest speaker leaves?
- What facts do we want to get from this person?
- What opinions would be interesting to have?
- Which of these questions are most important?
- How can we get an idea of this person's perspective on this kind of situation?
- Do you think this person will have a bias? What would it be? How can we find out?

Session 2: The Guest Speaker's Presentation

THINGS TO DO

1. Guest Speaker: The guest provides his/her information regarding the area of his/her expertise.
2. Students take notes and ask their questions.
3. Students should also be prepared to share with the guest speaker background on the problem and their decisions to date.

Session 3: Debriefing

THINGS TO DO

1. In a follow-up to the guest speaker, teacher and students should review the "Need to Know" board, removing questions which have been answered and adding new issues, if necessary.

2. Teachers and students should discuss the potential bias in the information provided by the guest speaker and the possible effects of that bias on the validity of the information.

THINGS TO ASK

- What were the things we learned from the guest speaker?
- How does the new information affect our thinking about the problem?
- Do we need to reorganize our approach to the problem?
- Did this person reveal a particular bias? If so, what?
- Where can we go to get another perspective? A balanced report of information?

ASSESSMENT

1. Students should report in their problem logs information provided by the guest lecturer and reflect on the potential of bias in the problem log.
2. Students write a thank-you letter to the guest speaker, detailing which information was particularly helpful.

NOTE TO TEACHER

If the expert comes to the classroom, all students can participate. This format can also be used by small groups who need to interview an outside expert outside of class; afterwards, they can report any new information to the class.

HANDOUT 6.1

VISITOR PLANNING SHEET

Student Name _____

Name of Visitor _____

Who is this visitor?

_____

_____

_____

Why is this visitor coming to see us?

_____

_____

Why is this visitor important to us?

_____

_____

_____

What would you like to tell our visitor about our problem?

_____

_____

What questions do you want to ask the visitor?

_____

_____

_____

lesson
7

The Algae Sub-Problem ✍️

LESSON LENGTH: 1 session

INSTRUCTIONAL PURPOSE

- To introduce students to the algae sub-problem.

MATERIALS AND HANDOUTS

Resource books about algae, pH, pollutants

Handout 7.1: "Need to Know" board
Handout 7.2: Algae sub-problem
Handout 7.3: Problem Log Questions

THINGS TO DO

1. Give students a copy of the sub-problem on Handout 7.1. Use the "Need to Know" board to clarify the new information and new questions which emerge from the sub-problem.

2. Divide learning responsibilities among students. Have students identify which information they would like to test experimentally (as a class or in small groups investigating different aspects of the problem).

THINGS TO ASK

- What new information does this scene give us?
- What do we need to know to understand what is going on?
- Why is Josh's mother concerned?
- What possible connections might you want to make?

- How would you like to go about finding out some of these things?
- Which information is best for outside research?
- Which information is best discovered through an experiment?
- Who could act as a resource person for us on this part of the problem?
- Does this scene make the problem change? How? Why not?

ASSESSMENT

1. Problem Log describing new areas of the problem.

HANDOUT 7.1

"NEED TO KNOW" BOARD

What do we know?	What do we need to know?	How can we find out?

The
Chesapeake
Bay

HANDOUT 7.2

ALGAL GROWTH

Josh, while gathering water samples in the river which borders his back yard, found some greenish slime, which his mother told him was algae. Josh's mother, a chemist, was upset that he had found algae "this far up the river." "No wonder the fish are dying," she said. Josh brought the sample in to school to analyze in the lab. What could this have to do with the problem?

HANDOUT 7.3

PROBLEM LOG QUESTIONS

Evaluate our problem statement based on this new information.

1. Would you like to change it or keep it the same? Why?

2. What changes would you make? Why?

Add the new information and new connections to your original problem web. Describe the changes you have made.

8

Salinity and Organisms

LESSON LENGTH: 2–4 sessions

INSTRUCTIONAL PURPOSE
- To investigate the effect of water on dried plant material.
- To investigate the impact of varying salinity on organisms.

NOTES TO TEACHER: (Pre-Activity)
1. Prepare a hay infusion in advance to guarantee viability of materials. Add a small clump of hay or other harvested grass to Mason jar of aged tap water, cover with cheesecloth to keep clean, put in lighted area undisturbed. Check water every day or two for presence of organisms. Use distilled water for the infusion if your water is very hard, soft, or treated. If you can't make an infusion, use pond water that has organisms in it.
2. Review use of hand lens or microscope. Discuss/review safety procedures for use of well slides and instruments.
3. The brine shrimp extension is useful because a saline solution is necessary for hatching and fresh water inhibits hatching and growth—which is different from what typically occurs in hay infusion.

MATERIALS AND HANDOUTS

Hay (can purchase through biological supply houses; use unsprayed dried materials—no herbicides or pesticides)

Hay infusions (different ages—1 day, 2 day, 3 day—whatever you can provide)

Eyedroppers, Good hand lens (1 per student if possible), Microscope (well slides, cover slips) (1 per team), Mason jar (clean glass jar approximately 1 quart size), Aged tap water (if very hard or treated, use distilled water), Cheesecloth for covering jar,

NaCl solutions (varying strengths—weak through strong—not iodized salt) (0.35%, 3.5 grams NaCl in 1 liter of water; 0.70%, 7 grams NaCl in 1 liter of water)

Water testing kit or salinity test (commercial or call outside expert such as county extension agent), Elodea (water plant available in most pet stores), Sprouts (grocery store)

Extension Materials:
    Brine shrimp eggs   Beakers or test tubes   Graduated cylinders

    Handout 8.1: Observations
    Handout 8.2: Hypothesis
    Handout 8.3: Problem Log Questions

THINGS TO DO

1. Have dried hay or grass available for student observation. Ask students to observe the dry material under a hand lens and draw what they see (Handout 8.1).

2. Provide the hay infusion for students to observe. Ask them to look at the liquid under a hand lens and microscope (low power) and draw and describe some of the organisms observed in the liquid (Handout 8.1). Ask them to hypothesize the source of the organisms.

   Extension: Ask them to identify at least 3 organisms they see and support their identification.

3. Ask the students to compare and contrast the organisms found in the different jars—according to age of infusion. Ask if amount of time impacts the amount or type of organism. Ask students how they would find that out. Ask student to design an experiment to investigate the above.

4. Determine a relationship between length of infusion time and number of organisms.

   Extension: Develop different infusions and compare results. Consider comparing findings with pond water or fish tank water. Have students e-mail students in different parts of the country and see if geographic location impacts organisms found . . . or if different materials (plains hay, suburban field grasses, salt hay, dry Spartina) all give the same results . . . or change types of water used to make infusions . . . or change temperatures.

5. Introduce the question of the effect of salinity on these organisms. Ask what happens if we introduce a salt solution into this environment. Have students record this hypothesis on Handout 8.2. Ask student to develop and experiment to investigate the impact of different salt solutions on the organisms found in hay infusions.

6. Determine salinity of original water used in infusion (teacher or student).

7. Using different solutions (varying salt concentrations) observe and record effect of salt solutions on organisms (Handout 8.2). Discuss results—compare team results in class. Discuss and/or conjecture on the possible reasons for the variations in the student results.

THINGS TO ASK

- Where do the organisms come from in the infusion?
- How did they get there?
- What does the water do to the hay?
- What impact does the amount of time in water have on the number and type of organism present?
- Does type of "hay" influence type of organisms? Why or why not? Does location of "hay" collection impact type of organisms? Why or why not?
- Where do "hay infusions" occur naturally?
- What happens to the organisms upon addition of different saline solutions?
- Where does this occur naturally?
- The salinity of the Bay varies throughout the year and according to location. What impact does this have on its organisms?

EXTENSIONS

Students should write up experiments that investigate the following:

Brine shrimp experiment: Use brine shrimp to investigate the impact of varying salinities on hatching and development.

Plant experiment: Use elodea or sprouts to investigate the impact of varying salinities on plants. (Note: One is a water plant, the other is not. How does this impact the results?)

Compare class results and discuss how brine shrimp and elodea are similar to bay organisms (food webs and system diagrams).

ASSESSMENT

1. Problem Log
2. Worksheet Review
3. Experiment review—written and performance

NOTE TO TEACHER

Remember to check guidelines for use of animal subjects prior to use of animals in any experiment. Discuss this requirement with students.

HANDOUT 8.1

OBSERVATIONS

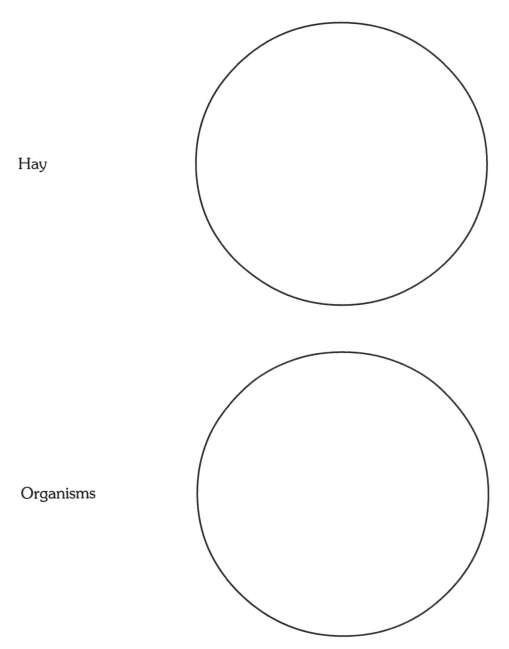

Hay

Organisms

If you have been able to identify some of these organisms, draw and identify each one on the back of this sheet.

Hypothesis:

Findings:

Original salinity of H_2O	Observed results on organisms
Salinity #1 Amount added: Concentration:	
Salinity #2 Amount added: Concentration:	
Salinity #3 Amount added: Concentration:	

1. Was your hypothesis correct?

2. What is the effect of different concentrations of salt solutions on the organisms?

3. What factors may have been overlooked when conducting this experiment?

4. How else might you test the effect of salinity on organisms?

5. What in your community is an example of a change in salinity occurring during the year (i.e., Where does this happen in real life)?

1. List and discuss how variations in salinity might occur naturally in the Bay.

2. How might they occur as a result of human-related activities?

3. What impacts on organisms might such natural and unnatural variations have on Bay organisms and why?

9

Field Trip to Local Aquatic Ecosystem

LESSON LENGTH: 4 sessions

INSTRUCTIONAL PURPOSE

- To collect field data and observe properties and elements of an aquatic ecosystem.

MATERIALS AND HANDOUTS

Water sampling kit (preferably one that tests **lots** of different things)
May be obtained through Carolina Biological Supply, 1-800-334-5551.
Sealable containers for water samples
Student notebooks and writing implements
Camera and film
VCR, camera and tape
pH indicator paper
Field guides to local aquatic organisms

A field guide is available from: *Fish and Wildlife Service*
Chesapeake Bay Estuary Program
180 Admiral Cochrane Drive, Suite 535
Annapolis, MD 21401

Handout 9.1: Field Trip Data Sheet
Handout 9.2: Problem Log Questions

Session 1: Planning

THINGS TO DO

1. Plan the field trip in class.

2. Before the field trip, introduce students to the water sampling kit. Assign groups of students to each test in the kit. Have them research the test and report to the class about the following:

a. How the test is performed

b. What the test measures

c. Why the test is important

3. Have students make their own data tables during the field trip preparation session.

Session 2: The Trip

1. On the field trip, before sampling the water, have students *write down their observations* about the body of water and describe the immediate locations of collection. Students should use field guides to identify as many of the plants and animals present as possible. Students should photograph things of interest.

2. Students should note:

   - Is the water turbid or clear?

   - Are there plants growing underwater (Submerged Aquatic Vegetation)?

   - Are there any aquatic animals present?

   - What is growing on the banks of the aquatic ecosystem?

3. Have students collect water samples from various locations and depths and use the water test kit to check for presence of ions (including the nutrients, phosphate, nitrate, and nitrite). Have them check water pH as well.

Session 3

1. Upon return to the classroom, show students how to use a hand lens or microscope to look at the water samples. Record observations about microscopic life that they observe.

2. Gather the same water sample data you did in the field (including a pH reading) on school tap water.

Session 4

1. Hold a debriefing session in which students report on their findings and the whole class analyzes the overall results.

2. Create a chart of group findings. What do they mean?

3. Review the videotape and photographs from the trip. Have students report and discuss their observations.

4. Have students complete the Problem Log Questions on Handout 9.2.

THINGS TO ASK

- What are the possible ranges of readings for each of the tests that were performed? What do the various readings tell you?

- How did the field results compare with the tap water results?

- How far from neutral was the pH? What does this mean?

- How diverse a collection of organisms was present? What does this tell you?

- How pervasive was the submerged aquatic vegetation?

- Was the water polluted?

- Are there any additional things you would want to observe or test if you could go back to the place we visited?

ASSESSMENT

1. Problem Log Questions.

2. Laboratory report indicating sampling results and their meaning.

NOTE TO TEACHER

You may want to contact your local fish and wildlife department for assistance in water testing. They may be able to test your samples on-site or in the classroom using electronic equipment.

HANDOUT 9.1

FIELD TRIP DATA SHEET

Name: _____

Date: _____

Water Sample # _____

Description of Site: _____

What does this indicate?

Presence of Submerged Aquatic Vegetation?

What does this indicate?

pH value: _____

What does this indicate?

Ion concentration:

      Phosphate: Reading: _____

                   Interpretation: _____

      Nitrate: Reading: _____

                   Interpretation: _____

      Nitrite: Reading: _____

                   Interpretation: _____

      Any others?

Salinity: Reading: _____

                Interpretation: _____

Can you make any conclusions about the water sample you tested? What?

What does today's field trip have to do with the problem? What can water sample tests tell us? Why might that information be valuable?

Based on the information we gained on the field trip, is the place we visited polluted? Why do you say this?

lesson 10

What Is the Effect of Fertilizer on Algal Growth?

LESSON LENGTH: 1 planning session; 1 session for experimental setup; observation time; 1 session for debriefing

INSTRUCTIONAL PURPOSE

- To allow students to plan and run an experiment designed to test the effect of fertilizer on the growth of algae.

MATERIALS AND HANDOUTS

Water testing kit

Fertilizer

Algae-filled water (either pond water or aquarium water)

Clean, chlorine-free water (either distilled water or tapwater that has been allowed to sit and release its chlorine into the air for a few days)

Containers for liquid (baby food jars are ideal): about five per group of students

Liquid measuring equipment: measuring cups, measuring spoons, pipets

pH paper

Handout 10.1: Student Brainstorming Worksheet

Handout 10.2: Student Experiment Worksheet

Handout 10.3: Student Protocol Worksheet

Handout 10.4: Laboratory Report Form

Session 1: Planning the Experiment

THINGS TO DO

1. Review the "Need to Know" Board.

2. Show students the materials for this lesson. Break students into small groups, and ask them to come up with a method for finding out what effect fertilizer has

on the growth of algae using the materials available. Pass out a copy of Handout 10.1 and have students complete it.

3. Discuss students' brainstorming results as a class.

4. Next, tell students that they need to design an experiment using their brainstorming ideas. Pass out copies of Handouts 10.2 and 10.3. Have students design their experiments and complete their Protocol Worksheets in their lab groups.

5. Check the protocols of each lab group. If the experiments look reasonable, allow students to set up and perform their experiments during the next session.

Sample Protocol

1. Prepare a stock solution of the fertilizer by adding 1 tablespoon of the fertilizer to one gallon of water.

2. To each of five baby food jars, add 20 ml of pond water and 20 ml of dechlorinated tapwater.

3. To the first baby food jar, add 1 teaspoon of the fertilizer stock solution; to the second baby food jar, add half teaspoon of the fertilizer stock solution; to the third baby food jar, add a quarter teaspoon of the fertilizer stock solution; and to the fourth baby food jar, add an eighth of a teaspoon of the fertilizer stock solution. Leave the last baby food jar alone.

4. Place the baby food jars in a sunny window. Each day for the next four days, observe the amount of algae in the jar and note your observations in the data table. Each day, photograph the jars for future reference. Each day, measure and record the pH of the water in each jar. If the water level in any of the jars drops, replace the water that has evaporated with fresh, dechlorinated tapwater.

5. Pool the results of each lab group into a class data table (thus assuring repeated trials). Analyze the results.

Session 2 and Observation Sessions

THINGS TO DO

During Session 2, students should set up their experiments. In order to give the algae time to grow, it would be advisable to schedule this session for a Monday and then allow students a short time for observation each day for the rest of the week.

Debriefing Session

THINGS TO DO

After students have run their experiments and made their observations, discuss their results as a class.

THINGS TO ASK

- What did low levels of fertilizer do to the algae?
- What did high levels of fertilizer do to the algae?
- Did the pH testing results vary between the jars that didn't get fertilizer and those that did?
- Thinking back to the lesson experimenting with variables, what other variables besides pH could be directly or indirectly affecting algae growth?
- What do you think would happen to a natural aquatic ecosystem that received small amounts of fertilizer from nearby farms?
- What do you think would happen to a nearby aquatic ecosystem that received large amounts of fertilizer from nearby farms?
- What other human activities could result in the entry of nutrients that would affect algal growth into the Bay?

ASSESSMENT

1. Experimental design forms.
2. Completed data tables.
3. Lab reports.

EXTENSIONS

Students could also design experiments that would test the effects of different kinds of fertilizer on algal growth (for example, high phosphate vs. low phosphate, organic vs. chemical); they could also look at other conditions that could potentially affect algal growth (temperature; presence of other kinds of pollutants).

HANDOUT 10.1

STUDENT BRAINSTORMING WORKSHEET

1. What do we need to find out? (What is the scientific problem?)

2. What materials do we have available?

3. How can we use these materials to help us find out?

4. What do we think will happen? (What is our hypothesis?)

5. What will we need to observe or measure in order to find out the answer to our scientific question?

Adapted from Cothron, J. G., Giese, R. N., & Rezba, R. J. (1989). *Students and research*. Dubuque, IA: Kendall/Hunt Publishing Co.

Title of Experiment:

Hypothesis (Educated guess about what will happen):

Independent Variable (The variable that **you change**):

Dependent Variable (The variable that responds to changes in the independent variable):

Observations/Measurements to Make:

Constants (All the things or factors that remain the same):

Control (The standard for comparing experimental effects):

The
Chesapeake
Bay

HANDOUT 10.3
STUDENT PROTOCOL WORKSHEET

1. List the materials you will need:

2. Write a step-by-step description of what you will do (like a recipe!). List every action you will take during the experiment.

3. What data will you be collecting?

4. Design a data table to collect and analyze your information.

HANDOUT 10.4

LABORATORY REPORT FORM

1. What did you do or test? (Include your experiment title)

2. How did you do it? What materials and methods did you use?

3. What did you find out? (Include a data summary and the explanation of its meaning)

4. What did you learn from your experiment?

5. What further questions do you now have?

6. Does the information you learned help with the problem?

lesson

11

The Pollution Sub-Problem

LENGTH OF LESSON: 1–2 sessions

INSTRUCTIONAL PURPOSE OVERALL UNIT GOALS

- To introduce students to sources of pollution in the Bay.

MATERIALS AND HANDOUTS

Resources about fertilizer and water pollution

Resources describing point and nonpoint sources of pollution

Handout 11.1: Newspaper ad "Bay Offenders"

Handout 11.2: Data sheet on Joshua Miller

Handout 11.3: Problem Log Questions

Session 1

THINGS TO DO

1. Give the newspaper ad to students (Handout 11.1). Have them identify familiar names (Joshua Miller, Julie and Josh's father). Use the "Need to Know" board to help students organize their questions about this new situation. Make sure that students "consider the source" and think about why the Bay Foundation would want to publish such an ad.

2. Students will ask for background information on Mr. Miller and the Miller farm. Inform students that you will gather specific information for them. In the meantime, have them start researching more general questions about farming and pollution.

THINGS TO ASK

- What's going on now?
- What does it say in the ad?
- Do these names mean anything to you?
- Why would the Bay Foundation want to publish this ad?
- Is the information reliable?
- What questions does this raise?
- What additional information do you want to have?
- Where you find answers to the new questions?

Session 2

THINGS TO DO

Present students with fact sheet on the Miller farm. Allow students to study the sheet and consider the new information. Ask students what they think is important on the fact sheet. Ask students to compare the general information about farming and pollution with the information on the fact sheet. They should hypothesize why Mr. Miller might be accused of being a Bay Offender, based on the new information. What from the farm could be contributing to the pollution in the Bay?

THINGS TO ASK

- Look at the sheet; what do you notice?
- What do you see that might be connected to Bay pollution?
- What would you like to do to test your hypothesis?
- If your hypothesis is right, what does it mean to Mr. Miller?
- What could he do to change his farming practice?
- What do you need to know now?
- How does this change your thinking about the problem?
- Would you redefine the problem based on this information? Why or why not? How?

- Are people responsible for nonprofit sources of pollution as "guilty" of damaging the environment as are those responsible for point sources? Why? Why not?
- Are there legal implications apparent from the nature of the offenses? What might they be?

ASSESSMENT

Problem Log activity: Problem re-definition and rationale.

NOTE TO TEACHER

If students do not make the Bay-farm connection right away, go back to more generic questions of farming and pollution. Continue this line of questioning until students find the connection. Have helpful resources available for follow-up.

Hampton Area Times, January 3, Sec. C

ARE *YOU* A BAY OFFENDER???

The beautiful Chesapeake Bay is also dangerous. And dying. Every day poisonous pollutants enter the waters of the Bay, endangering the wildlife and balance of nature.

People, too, are being affected. Each year more and more local fishermen and women are forced to close their family businesses because of the diminished supply of seafood in the Bay. Every individual is responsible for the condition of the Bay, and and we think that it's time that people take responsibility for their actions. For the next three weeks we will be publishing lists of the major offenders in our area.

Are **YOU** on this list? What are you going to do to help save this precious natural resource?

BAY OFFENDERS:

Jane Bessemer	Owner, Bessemer's Garden Supplies
Lee Ward	Director, St. Francis Hospital
Steve Boyce	Farmer
Mark Bailey	Anchor Industries
Joshua Miller	Farmer
Megan Peterson	CEO, Fresh! Cola
Kris Workman	Manager, Nature's Dairy Products

IT'S TIME TO CHANGE YOUR WAYS!!!

*Ad paid for by the Bay Today! Society

The
Chesapeake
Bay

HANDOUT 11.2

DATA SHEET ON JOSHUA MILLER

Bay Today!
555 Chesapeake Place
Hampton, Virginia 23118
(804) 555-2322   FAX 804-555-2362

Fact Sheet

Name: Joshua Miller, Sr.

Occupation: Farmer

Description: A large family farm in Charles City County, bordering on the James River. Products yielded from the farm include corn and wheat. Heavy use of nitrogen fertilizer on crops. Spray dusting and direct application employed. 1,000 acres farmed annually, with an additional rotating 250 acres to lie fallow. No dairy products produced for distribution on the farm, although cows are kept for family use.

Decision: Definitely a nonpoint source!

HANDOUT 11.3

PROBLEM LOG QUESTIONS

A lot of new information emerged in today's discussion. Analyze this information and decide whether or not the problem has changed enough that our original statement needs to be changed. If you think it needs to be changed, say why; if not, state why not. What are your new ideas for a problem statement?

Has the problem changed? How?

Should we change our statement? Why?

New problem statement:

lesson 12

The Economic Sub-Problem

LESSON LENGTH: 2–4 sessions

INSTRUCTIONAL PURPOSE

- To introduce students to the economic issues connected with the Bay pollution problem.

MATERIALS AND HANDOUTS

Resource materials on:

      economics

      farming

      fertilizer and pollution

      jobs associated with the Bay

Handout 12.1: Argument Sheet

    Handout 12.2: Sub-Problem introducing argument between Josh and his father

Handout 12.3: Problem Log Questions

Sessions 1–2

THINGS TO DO

1. Present the sub-problem describing Josh's distress over his argument with his father about the use of fertilizer. Use the "Need to Know" board, if necessary, to identify what information students need to have to decide which side they support. This may include finding out more about what would happen to the Miller farm if Mr. Miller used other kinds of fertilizer or no fertilizer.

2. Have students view and read the picture book *Bay Shore Park: The Death and Life of an Amusement Park* by Victoria Crenson (1995) and published by W.H. Freeman. Ask them to reflect on what perspectives it provides on the Bay problem.

THINGS TO ASK

- Josh seems pretty upset. Is his response reasonable?
- What are the facts supporting Josh's point of view?
- What are the facts supporting Mr. Miller's point of view?
- What else do you think you want to find out before you decide which point of view you would support?
- Are Mr. Miller's claims justified?
- What are the different elements of his argument?
- What other stakeholders might make the same argument as Mr. Miller? Why?
- Do you feel capable of making a decision about this right now? Would you like more information?
- About what?

Sessions 3–4

THINGS TO DO

Have students identify the appealing aspects of both sides of the argument—keeping the family farm, keeping the prices of food down versus keeping the fishing industry and its associated jobs going, saving the life of the Bay. Ask students what should be done when two appealing sides oppose each other.

THINGS TO ASK

- Is either point of view unreasonable? Is either argument wrong?
- Does Josh's father have a right to operate the farm the way he does?
- Do the Bay fishermen have a right to operate their businesses?
- Does the Bay wildlife have a right to clean waters?
- Do the "rights" of animals exist on a level parallel to the "rights" of humans?
- Look at your list of appeals. Which of the appeals is operating in your response?

ASSESSMENT

1. Student's description of ethical appeals.
2. Quality of background research for classroom discussion.
3. Synthesis of arguments and rationale for position selected in problem log.

NOTE TO TEACHER

A local farmer or agricultural extension agent would be a good guest speaker or "telephone mentor" for this issue; an economist could be brought in to present basic information about cost/benefit arguments.

The Chesapeake Bay

HANDOUT 12.1

ARGUMENT SHEET

Arguments Supporting Bay Supporters	Arguments Supporting Farmers

Draw a line connecting the issues which the two groups share in common.

Draw a circle around issues which are directly contradictory to the other side and connect the contradicting items with a line.

HANDOUT 12.2

JOSH AND MR. MILLER

Josh came into class today visibly upset. You noticed as he passed you in the hall this morning that his eyes were red. All through your class on cell structure and mitosis he kept his head on his desk.

After class you asked Josh to stay behind. When you asked Josh what was wrong, he said he had an argument with his father over the use of fertilizer on the farm. Josh reported to his father what he had learned with you about the effects of runoff on the waters of the James River and the Chesapeake Bay. To his surprise, Josh's father was aware of the pollution problem but wasn't going to change his farming strategies.

"I can't afford to change, son," he said. "What with the price of organic fertilizer and the price of other people's crops, we'd be out of business in two years."

Josh was hurt and outraged at his father's "lack of ethics." He has asked you to call his father and try to change his mind.

What are you going to do?

NOTE TO TEACHER

See Part III for suggestions about where to obtain an ordinance or legislative document for your area.

Session 3

THINGS TO DO

Introduce students to the six ethical appeals (see Handout 13.8). Discuss the appeals and how they might affect how students see their roles.

THINGS TO ASK

- Which of the appeals is most suited to your group's position?
- What other appeals should they be considering?
- How can those other appeals be addressed?
- Are all of the appeals important?
- Are some more important than others?
- Do particular appeals seem to be the "given realm" of distinct constituent groups?

Session 4

Debate various resolutions to the problem. Invite some of your guest speakers back to be Town Council members or appoint students to the role. Have students present and defend their position before the Council. Send a copy of the ordinance to representatives from different constituent groups so that students can have the benefit of their reactions.

Session 5

THINGS TO DO

1. Have students discuss whether or not they thought they were successful in creating a "good" problem resolution.

2. Ask students to present group results from studying the ethical appeals. Discuss as a whole group.

3. Ask students to complete Problem Log Questions (Handout 13.9).

THINGS TO ASK

- What will the short- and long-range consequences of your resolution be?

- Who will be directly affected? Who will be affected indirectly?

ASSESSMENT

All facets of problem resolution work may be used to assess student learning.

HANDOUT 13.1
ROLE SHEET

Ecologist

You are a resident of the county. You are very upset by the algal bloom in the river next to the county and know what that means to aquatic life in the James River. You are in favor of the ordinance because you know that something has to be done to end this pollution of our resources.

Chair, County Board of Supervisors

You are a good citizen who ran for chair of the Board because you care about your community and want it to have a good future in all ways possible. You understand the need for the ordinance, but you also understand the fears and concerns of your citizens. You want to do what is best for the county.

Developer

You have just bought fifty acres of prime waterfront land. You plan to develop a resort complex complete with a marina, condos, and a waterfront golf course. The ordinance would spoil your plans and you would be stuck with fifty unusable acres of land, in your opinion.

HANDOUT 13.4
ROLE SHEET

Local Landowner

You are opposed to any ordinances restricting land use. You think that your property will lose its value and you will lose money when you sell it. You are angry because you think the state is always taking things away from citizens without paying for them. You need the money to pay for college for your child.

Chesapeake Bay Local Assistance Dept. Staff Member

You want an ordinance passed that will follow the requirements of the Chesapeake Bay Preservation Acts. You realize that it scares many landowners and want to educate them about best management practices and about how easy and inexpensive they are to use.

Citizen of the County

You are a life-long resident of the community. When you were young, you used to fish and crab in the James River. Now those areas are off-limits due to pollution. You work at the Newport News Shipyard. You want the pollution to end but want the county to do well economically.

Mr. Miller

You are a farmer in the community. You oppose any law that will make you control non-point source pollution. You think that it would cost too much to change fertilizers and would eventually put you out of business. You would change, however, if someone would find a cheap way of doing so.

SIX MAJOR ETHICAL APPEALS

APPEAL TO JUSTICE

Do the consequences justify the action?

APPEAL TO CONSEQUENCES

Will the action result in the desired behaviors or results for all parties? Is it likely that the desired consequences will occur? Is the consequence valuable? Will the consequence have a wide impact?

APPEAL TO RIGHTS

Is the person entitled as a part of individual liberties (rights guaranteed by law which can be waived by the individual but not removed by other individuals).

APPEAL TO COST EFFECTIVENESS

Is the result worth the money it requires? Does this represent a worthwhile expenditure of public or personal funds? Costs here include human labor cost as well as financial cost at the macro level (cost to society).

APPEAL TO VIRTUES

Does the action remain constant with the belief system espoused by the group or does it violate basic values (integrity, compassion, courage, honesty)?

APPEAL TO PERSONHOOD

Does the action promote or diminish the quality of life for constituent parties?

PROBLEM LOG QUESTIONS

Our government was built around the idea that checks and balances are necessary to ensure that all groups will be equally represented. However, sometimes this means that in trying to please everyone we please no one. Relate these ideas to your experience in debating the various resolutions at the Town Council.

Bay Fest

LESSON LENGTH: 1 session Bay Fest preceded by two weeks of preparation.

INSTRUCTIONAL PURPOSE

- To give students an opportunity to synthesize and integrate the information they have learned throughout the Bay Unit.

MATERIALS AND HANDOUTS

Invitations to Parents/School/Community

Poster board, chart paper, graph paper, markers, artifacts, etc. to support student presentations

Handout 14.1: Bay Fest Planning Sheet

Handout 14.2: Persuasive Speech Assessment Form

THINGS TO DO

1. As the class reaches closure on the Bay problem, a group planning/brainstorming session can be held to discuss how to present all of the learning activities students completed during the unit. A review of the areas of investigation that led to the resolution might be an appropriate beginning.

2. A board chart can be created listing all areas of investigation that contributed to the understanding of the problem. The list can then be divided among individuals or small groups of students who will take responsibility for presenting that information at the Bay Fest celebration.

3. Individual and/or small groups of students can be responsible for presenting specific parts of the unit to the public. They can be encouraged to develop reports, displays, graphs, charts, pictures, models, etc.

4. Ideas may include (but should not be limited to):

- Presentation on the sea trout problem: why it was important
- Models of the Bay watershed
- Model of an ecologically safe farm
- Water flow models
- Displays of science experiments performed in the unit
- Opinion poll results
- Suggested regulatory ordinance
- Speeches supporting and not supporting Bay regulation
- Panel discussion of central issues
- Charts and demonstrations of all related unit products

THINGS TO ASK

- What parts of the investigation do you think people ought to see?
- What information is critical for them to know in order to understand the diminished supply of sea trout?
- Why is this information important?
- What would be the best way to communicate these results?
- Which would be best presented visually? Which through oral presentations?

ASSESSMENT

Student presentations using the form in Handout 14.2.

HANDOUT 14.1

BAY FEST PLANNING SHEET

Name: _____

Presentation Topic: _____

Things I know about this topic:

Things I still want to find out:

The "big ideas" to get across to the audience:

The connections I want to make:

How the information about this topic contributed to problem resolution:

What are some interesting ways I can present this information to others?

What materials will I need in order to best present my information?

HANDOUT 14.2

PERSUASIVE SPEECH ASSESSMENT FORM

Name: _____ Date: _____

Use the following rating scale to evaluate each quality:

        1 = Needs Improvement

        2 = Adequate

        3 = Excellent

_____ The purpose of the speech was clear.

_____ The speaker's reasoning was clear and logical.

_____ The basic components of the argument were evident.

_____ The speaker showed knowledge of the subject.

_____ The speaker addressed opposing points of view.

_____ The speaker was audible, maintained eye contact, and spoke with expression.

_____ The speaker held the interest of the audience.

The best part of this speech was:

A suggestion for improvement is:

lesson 15

Final Overall Unit Assessment Activity

INSTRUCTIONAL PURPOSE

- To assess understanding of the scientific content taught by this unit.
- To assess the ability of the student to use appropriate scientific process skills in the resolution of a real-world problem.
- To assess student understanding of the concept of systems.

ESTIMATED TIME

The content assessment should take the students approximately thirty minutes; the experimental design assessment should take the students approximately thirty minutes; and the systems assessment should take the students approximately thirty minutes.

MATERIALS AND HANDOUTS

Handout 15.1: Final Content Assessment

Handout 15.2: Experimental Design Assessment

Handout 15.3: Systems Assessment

Scoring protocols for Final Content Assessment, Experimental Design Assessment, and Systems Assessment

PROCEDURE

Have students complete assessments found in Handouts 15.1, 15.2, and 15.3.

1. When the first European settlers arrived, the Chesapeake Bay was rich in wildlife. Many oysters in the Bay were so old that they had grown to an immense size: some were over a foot long. Today, the number of oysters is much lower than when the settlers came, and they are much smaller.

   a. Why do you think the number of oysters has decreased?

   b. Why do you think that the oysters that are left are smaller than the ones that were in the Bay when the first settlers came?

2. Both biotic and abiotic factors are important in the Bay ecosystem.

   a. Name one abiotic factor and describe its importance to the Bay.

   b. Name one biotic factor and describe its importance to the Bay.

3. Global warming, which is thought by many scientists to be occurring as a result of human production of carbon dioxide and other greenhouse gases, is expected to result in the melting of polar ice and an increase in sea level worldwide.

   a. What effects would you expect this increase in sea level to have on the Bay's boundaries?

   b. What effects would you expect this increase in sea level to have on the Bay's salinity?

4. Why would each of the two effects listed in problem 3 above potentially be important to the organisms that live in and around the Bay?

   a. Boundary changes:

   b. Salinity:

5. Everyone that lives in the watershed that feeds the Chesapeake Bay affects the Bay ecosystem. Suppose you lived in the suburbs near the Chesapeake Bay and had a lawn and a garden. Describe one thing that you could do to help the Bay ecosystem survive, and explain why that one thing could help.

EXPERIMENTAL DESIGN ASSESSMENT (30 MINUTES)

You are at summer camp. This evening all the campers are sitting around the campfire, roasting marshmallows and slapping mosquitoes. It has rained a lot this summer and the mosquitoes are a real nuisance. One of your friends tells the group that he never gets bitten because he always wears black, and mosquitoes hate to bite people who wear black. You notice that he hasn't gotten any mosquito bites tonight; you are wearing red and have fourteen new bites. You decide that maybe it would be worth doing an experiment to see if your friend is right. Everyone in your group has black T-shirts and shorts, so the supply of black clothing isn't a problem.

What experiment could you do to see whether your friend is right? In your answer, include the following:

  a. Your hypothesis:

  b. The materials you would need:

  c. The protocol you would use:

  d. A data table showing what data you would collect:

  e. A description of how you would use your data to decide whether mosquitoes don't like to bite people who are wearing black.

HANDOUT 15.3

SYSTEMS ASSESSMENT (30 MINUTES)

A pond can be thought of as a system. For this system, do the following:

1. List the parts of the system. Include boundaries, elements, input, and output.

   Boundaries:

   Elements:

   Input:

   Output:

2. Draw a diagram of the system that shows where each of the parts can be found.

3. On your diagram, draw lines (in a different color) showing three important interactions between different parts of the system. Why is each of these interactions important to the system? Explain your answer.

   a. Interaction #1:

   b. Interaction #2:

   c. Interaction #3:

SCORING PROTOCOL
Final Content Assessment

1. **(10 points)** When the first European settlers arrived, the Chesapeake Bay was rich in wildlife. Many oysters in the Bay were so old that they had grown to an immense size: some were over a foot long. Today, the number of oysters is much lower than when the settlers came, and they are much smaller.

   a. **(5 points)** Why do you think the number of oysters has decreased?

   There are more people harvesting oysters than there were when the settlers came, so there are fewer oysters left to breed and the population is smaller; in addition, human activities have reduced the available oyster habitat and introduced oyster diseases which further reduce the oyster population.

   Scoring: accept any of the following possibilities: habitat destruction, disease, and/or overharvesting.

   b. **(5 points)** Why do you think that the oysters that are left are smaller than the ones that were in the Bay when the first settlers came?

   The really large oysters were very old, in oyster terms: oysters continue to grow throughout their lifetime. Before the settlers came, many oysters were left undisturbed and grew to a ripe old age; after the settlers came, so many oysters were harvested from the Bay that very few had an opportunity to grow to a large size. Now the oysters are much smaller.

2. **(10 points)** Both biotic and abiotic factors are important in the Bay ecosystem.

   a. **(5 points)** Name one abiotic factor and describe its importance to the Bay.

   Possibilities include: salinity, weather, tidal forces, turbidity of the water, water temperature, nutrient load.

   Scoring: give five points for any reasonable answer and explanation

   b. **(5 points)** Name one biotic factor and describe its importance to the Bay.

   Possibilities include: submerged aquatic vegetation, algal growth, all animal populations.

   Scoring: give five points for any reasonable answer and explanation

3. **(10 points)** Global warming, which is thought by many scientists to be occurring as a result of human production of carbon dioxide and other greenhouse gases, is expected to result in the melting of polar ice and an increase in sea level worldwide.

   a. **(5 points)** What effects would you expect this increase in sea level to have on the Bay's boundaries?

The Bay's boundaries would move, with areas that had formerly been above water becoming underwater.

b. **(5 points)** What effects would you expect this increase in sea level to have on the Bay's salinity?

The salinity in different parts of the Bay depends on the amount of seawater present. With increased sea levels, the salinity in the estuaries around the main part of the Bay, as well as in the Bay itself, would increase.

4. **(10 points)** Why would each of the two effects listed in problem 3 above potentially be important to the organisms that live in and around the Bay?

a. **(5 points)** Boundary changes:

Water level increases would alter the habitats of many of the organisms living along the shores of the Bay. New marshes might be created, while previously shallow areas might become too deep for their inhabitants to tolerate.

b. **(5 points)** Salinity:

Organisms that required low salinity and were incapable of moving (such as freshwater mussels in the streams that feed the Bay) would die as the salinity increased; other organisms that could tolerate higher salinity would move in to take their place.

Scoring: accept any answer that lists plausible effects from each of the two factors listed above; give five points for each explanation.

5. **(10 points)** Everyone that lives in the watershed that feeds the Chesapeake Bay affects the Bay ecosystem. Suppose you lived in the suburbs near the Chesapeake Bay and had a lawn and a garden. Describe one thing that you could do to help the Bay ecosystem survive, and explain why that one thing could help.

Possibilities include: use less fertilizer on the lawn so that excess fertilizer doesn't run into the Bay; plow up some of the lawn and plant plants that are more useful to wildlife; don't use pesticides on the lawn and garden so that the residues don't end up in the Bay; make sure that your garden doesn't release sediment into the runoff from your property; plant things that native organisms can use as shelter or food (for example, food for a native species of butterfly or bird).

Give ten points for each reasonable answer and explanation.

Note: "Recycling" is not a particularly good answer to the question posed above, unless the student makes an *explicit* connection between something like recycling paper and the consequent reduced need for paper from the paper mills located along the shore of the Bay.

Total number of points possible: 50

SCORING PROTOCOL

Experimental Design Assessment

You are at summer camp. This evening all the campers are sitting around the campfire, roasting marshmallows and slapping mosquitoes. It has rained a lot this summer and the mosquitoes are a real nuisance. One of your friends tells the group that he never gets bitten because he always wears black, and mosquitoes hate to bite people who wear black. You notice that he hasn't gotten any mosquito bites tonight; you are wearing red and have fourteen new bites. You decide that maybe it would be worth doing an experiment to see if your friend is right. Everyone in your group has black T-shirts and shorts, so the supply of black clothing isn't a problem. What experiment could you do to see whether your friend is right?

In your answer, include the following:

a. **(5 points)** Your hypothesis:

> Mosquitoes don't like to bite people who are wearing black.

> (Note: other hypotheses are possible; accept all reasonable answers; give five points for any reasonable hypothesis.)

b. **(10 points)** The materials you would need, including any necessary safety equipment:

> (*Sample* answer)
> Campers
> Black T-shirts and shorts
> T-shirts and shorts of other colors

> (Note: This materials list does not need to be comprehensive. Accept all reasonable materials lists, as long as they're consonant with the hypothesis.)

c. **(10 points)** The protocol you would use:

> (*Sample* answer) I would have everyone in the group get his/her black T-shirt and return to the campfire. Before the experiment began, I would have everyone color their existing mosquito bites red with a felt tip pen so that old bites wouldn't be counted as new ones. I would then have half the group put on their black T-shirts and shorts, while the other half of the group put on T-shirts and shorts of other colors. I would give the mosquitoes half an hour to bite, and then I would have each person count their new bites, record the number, and color the bites green with a felt-tip pen, so that the number could be re-checked if necessary. I would then have the group that had been wearing black change to clothing of other colors, while the group that had been wearing non-black clothes changed to black ones. After half an hour, we would again count new bites and record the numbers; this time we would color the new bites blue with a felt-tip pen. If there was

confusion about the data, we could recount each person's green and blue spots to be sure that the original count was accurate. Switching the groups would serve to eliminate any possible bias in the data caused by mosquito preferences for other things about their victims. The people wearing non-black clothing serve as a positive control: we know that the mosquitoes are biting tonight, so if these people don't get any new bites, then the experiment has gone sour and should be repeated on a night when the mosquitoes are biting better.

Scoring: Give five points for any reasonable protocol (or experimental outline: not every step need be listed in fine detail, but it should be clear what the student intends to test) that is consonant with the hypothesis given (if the two seem to be unrelated, withhold these points); give five points for the presence of a control (not necessarily labeled as such) for the experiment.

d. **(15 points)** A data table showing what data you would collect:

Victim's name	Number of bites when wearing	
	Black	Other color

Scoring: Give five points for the presence of a data table; 5 points if there is an independent variable (not necessarily labeled as such) present in the data table headings; and five points if there is at least one dependent variable (not necessarily labeled as such) present in the data table headings. In this answer, clothing color is the independent variable, and number of bites is the dependent variable.

(Note: accept all reasonable answers, as long as they're consonant with the student's answers to parts a–d.)

e. **(10 points)** A description of how you would use your data to decide whether mosquitoes don't like to bite people who are wearing black.

I would compare the average number of bites gotten by people when they were wearing black to the average number of bites gotten by people who were wearing other colors and see if these numbers were significantly different. If the average number of bites gotten by people when they were wearing black was significantly smaller than the average number of bites gotten by people when they were wearing other colors, I would say that the hypothesis was correct.

Scoring: Give ten points for an answer that explains how the data will be used to come up with a conclusion. If the student doesn't mention the data, then give no points.

(Note: accept all reasonable answers, as long as they're consonant with the student's answers to parts a–d.)

Total number of points possible: 50

SCORING PROTOCOL
Systems Assessment

A pond can be thought of as a system. For this system, do the following:

1. **(25 points total)** List the parts of the system. Include boundaries, elements, input, and output.

   - *Boundaries (describe)*:
   Sample answer: the boundaries would include the shoreline, the bottom and sides of the pond (the mud would be considered a part of the pond), and the surface of the water.

   Scoring: For ten points, accept any reasonable *closed* boundaries.

   - *Elements* (List at least five):
   Elements could include water, microorganisms, dissolved gases, plants, animals.

   Scoring: Give one point for each reasonable element consistent with the boundaries up to a maximum of five points.

   - *Input* (List at least two kinds):
   Rainwater, dust, water from whatever source feeds the pond (if there is one).

   Scoring: Give 2.5 points for each listed input item consistent with the boundaries up to a maximum of five points.

   - *Output* (List at least two kinds):
   Water vapor, carbon dioxide from the pond animals, oxygen from the pond plants, creatures leaving the pond, etc.

   Scoring: Give 2.5 points for each listed output item consistent with the boundaries, up to five points.

2. **(10 points)** Draw a diagram of the system that shows where each of the parts can be found.

   Scoring: Accept any reasonable diagram that includes the system components listed in the answer to question 1.

3. **(15 points total)** On your diagram, draw lines (in a different color) showing three important interactions between different parts of the system. Why is each of these interactions important to the system? Explain your answer.

(Accept any reasonable interaction; give five points for each correct answer.) Examples are given below.

a. Interaction #1:

Dust from the air includes algal spores which can germinate once they enter the pond: pond water and spores interact.

b. Interaction #2:

Predator-prey relationships within the pond (fish eating mosquito larvae and so on).

c. Interaction #3:

Plants producing oxygen and sugar as a result of solar energy input into the pond.

Total number of points possible: 50

Part III

REFERENCES

REFERENCES

City of Hampton. *Hampton citizen's guide to environmental services.* Hampton, VA: City of Hampton.

Cothron, J.H., Giese, R.N., & Rezba, R.J. (1996). *Science experiments and projects for students.* Dubuque, IA: Kendall/Hunt Publishing Company.

Cothron, J.H., Giese, R.N., & Rezba, R.J. (1996). *Science experiments by the hundreds.* Dubuque, IA: Kendall/Hunt Publishing Company.

Cothron, J.H., Giese, R.N., & Rezba, R.J. (1996). *Students and research: Practical strategies for science classrooms and competition.* Dubuque, IA: Kendall/Hunt Publishing Company.

National Geographic Society (1993). *Water: The power, promise, and turmoil of North America's fresh water.* Washington, DC: National Geographic Society.

Smith, R.L. (1986). *Elements of Ecology* (2nd Ed.). NY: Harper & Row.

Modular units that may be integrated with *The Chesapeake Bay Ecosystem*

- Mapping Fish Habitats (Grades 6–10)

- Global Warming and the Greenhouse Effect (Grades 7–10)
  Available from:
  Great Explorations in Math & Science (GEMS)
  Lawrence Hall of Science
  University of California
  Berkeley, CA 94720-5200
  (510) 642-7771

- Ecosystems (Grade 5)
  Developed by:
  Science and Technology for Children (STC)
  Distributed by:
  Carolina Biological Supply
  2700 York Road
  Burlington, NC 27215
  (800) 334-5551

- Environments (Grades 5–6)
  Developed by:
  Full Options Science Systems (FOSS)
  Distributed by:
  Britannica Educational Corporation
  310 S. Michigan Avenue, 6th Floor
  Chicago, IL 60604
  (800) 554-9862

- Stream Tables

- Water Flow
  Developed by:
  Elementary Science Study (ESS)
  Distributed by:
  Delta Education
  P.O. Box 915
  Hudson, NH 03051-0915
  (800) 258-1302

- The Waste Hierarchy

- Investigating Groundwater
  Developed by:
  CEPUP, Lawrence Hall of Science
  Distributed by:
  Innovative Learning Publications (Addison-Wesley)
  Route 128
  Reading, MA 01867
  (800) 552-2259

- There is No Away (Grade 6)
  Developed and Distributed by:
  Insights
  Education Development Center, Inc.
  55 Chapel Street
  Newton, MA 02160
  (800) 225-4276

Numerous resources are available to get up-to-date information on the Chesapeake Bay and current legislation that affects the Bay. The following are intended to be suggestions as starting points.

LEGISLATION

- Virginia Wetlands Act of 1972
- Congressional Clean Water Act amended in 1987
- Clean Air Act (federal)
- Chesapeake Bay Preservation Act (Virginia)
  Local Assistance Department
  (800) 243-7229

- Chesapeake Bay Critical Area Act (Maryland)
  Maryland Critical Area Commission
  45 Calvert Street, Annapolis, MD 21401
  (410) 974-2426

- Chesapeake Bay Commission—a group that assists states in their legislative efforts to protect the Chesapeake Bay. They publish an annual report that summarizes all legislation relevant to the Bay.
  60 West Street, Suite 200, Annapolis, MD 21401
  (410) 263-3420

ELECTRONIC RESOURCES

- BIOS (Basin-wide Information On-line Service) provides background information, news and factsheets on the Chesapeake Bay
  http://www.gmu.edu/bios

- Virginia Institute of Marine Science
  http://www.vims.edu

OTHER RESOURCES FOR INFORMATION:

- Chesapeake Bay Foundation
  162 Prince George St.
  Annapolis, MD 21401
  (410) 268-8816

- Chesapeake Bay Program Office
  (part of the EPA; maintains an extensive library)
  410 Severn Avenue, Suite 109
  Annapolis, MD 21403
  (800) 968-7229
  http://www.epa.gov/r3chespk/
  (410) 267-5701 (Dr. Barbara Callahan)

- Chesapeake Bay Regional Information Service (a service provided by the Alliance for The Chesapeake Bay)
  (800) 662-CRIS

- Virginia Institute of Marine Science
  P.O. Box 1346
  Gloucester Point, VA 23062
  (804) 642-7000

- U.S. Fish and Wildlife Service

- U.S. Environmental Protection Agency

- State Department of Environmental Quality

- Cooperative Extension Service

- Local Environmental Relations Office

A good source of materials is:
Save the Bay Shop
188 Main Street
Annapolis, MD 21401
(410) 268-8832
FAX (410) 268-8832

They carry a number of books, field guides, and videos. Of particular interest is a Landsat photo of the Bay that is made into a poster.

An overview of the outstanding titles available from the

CENTER FOR GIFTED EDUCATION

SCIENCE

A PROBLEM-BASED LEARNING SYSTEM FROM THE CENTER FOR GIFTED EDUCATION FOR YOUR K-8 SCIENCE LEARNERS

The Center for Gifted Education has seven curriculum units containing different real-world situations that face today's society, plus a guide to using the curriculum. The units are geared towards different elementary levels, yet can be adapted for use in all levels of K-8.

The goal of each unit is to allow students to analyze several real-world problems, understand the concept of systems, and conduct scientific experiments. These units also allow students to explore various scientific topics and identify meaningful problems for investigation.

Through these units your students experience the work of real science in applying data-handling skills, analyzing information, evaluating results, and learning to communicate their understanding to others.

LANGUAGE ARTS

A LANGUAGE ARTS CURRICULUM FROM THE CENTER FOR GIFTED EDUCATION FOR YOUR GRADES 2-11

The Center for Gifted Education at the College of William and Mary has developed a series of language arts curriculum units for high-ability learners.

The goals of each unit are to develop students' skills in literature interpretation and analysis, persuasive writing, linguistic competency, and oral communication, as well as to strengthen students' reasoning skills and understanding of the concept of change.

The units engage students in exploring carefully selected, challenging works of literature from various times, cultures, and genres, and encourage students to reflect on the readings through writing and discussion.

The units also provide numerous opportunities for students to explore interdisciplinary connections to language arts and to conduct research around issues relevant to their own lives. A guide to using the curriculum is also available.